THE BOOK

D0358298

HAPPINESS

LIZZIE CORNWALL

summersdale

THE BOOK OF HAPPINESS

Summersdale Publishers Ltd
46 West Street
Chichester
West Sussex
PO19 1RP
UK

www.summersdale.com

Printed and bound in China

ISBN: 978-1-84953-761-2

Substantial discounts on bulk quantities of Summersdale books are available to corporations, professional associations and other organisations. For details contact Nicky Douglas by telephone: +44 (0) 1243 756902, fax: +44 (0) 1243 786300 or email: nicky@summersdale.com.

To..

From..

It is always the simple that produces the marvellous.

Amelia Barr

LOOK FOR THE SILVER
LININGS IN LIFE.

Laugh and the world laughs with you.

Ella Wheeler Wilcox

BE OPEN TO THE
POSSIBILITY OF
MIRACLES.

SMILE. SMILING RELEASES
ENDORPHINS, THE BODY'S
NATURAL FEEL-GOOD DRUG!

Wherever you go, no matter what the weather, always bring your own sunshine.

Anthony J. D'Angelo

To be without some of
the things you want is an
indispensable part of happiness.

Bertrand Russell

SCIENTISTS HAVE FOUND
BRIGHTER CLOTHES MAKE YOU
HAPPIER. PUT ON YOUR MOST
COLOURFUL OUTFIT TODAY!

Look at everything as though
you were seeing it either for
the first or last time.

Betty Smith

Turn your face to the sun and the shadows fall behind you.

Maori proverb

DANCE TO YOUR OWN BEAT!

Dwell on the beauty of life.
Watch the stars, and see
yourself running with them.

Marcus Aurelius

Mix a little foolishness with
your serious plans. It is lovely
to be silly at the right moment.

Horace

NEW DAY.
FRESH START.

SPEND TIME WITH CHILDREN.
THEY ARE THE EXPERTS ON
LAUGHING, PLAYING AND
TAKING LIFE LIGHTLY.

A happy life consists not in the absence, but in the mastery of hardships.

Helen Keller

Feelings are much like
waves, we can't stop them from
coming but we can choose
which one to surf.

Jonatan Mårtensson

KEEP YOUR FAVOURITE
INSPIRING QUOTE ON A PIECE
OF PAPER IN YOUR WALLET
AND READ IT THROUGHOUT
THE DAY.

For myself I am an optimist –
it does not seem to be much
use being anything else.

Winston Churchill

Laughter is the sound
of the soul dancing.

Jarod Kintz

HAPPINESS IS
HOME-MADE.

Too much of a good thing
can be wonderful.

Mae West

Wherever you go,
go with all your heart.

Confucius

KEEP PHOTOS OF FAMILY AND FRIENDS NEARBY SO YOU FEEL SURROUNDED BY LOVE DURING THE DAY.

DO MORE OF WHAT MAKES YOU HAPPY.

Think big thoughts but
relish small pleasures.

H. Jackson Brown Jr

You only get one
chance at life and you
have to grab it boldly.

Bear Grylls

IF IT RAINS, PUT
YOUR WELLIES ON AND
SEE HOW MANY PUDDLES
YOU CAN JUMP IN.

May you live every day of your life.

Jonathan Swift

START YOUR DAY BY
LETTING GO OF EXPECTATIONS.
EMBRACE EVERYTHING THAT
COMES YOUR WAY.

Remember that happiness is a way of travel, not a destination.

Roy M. Goodman

The purpose of dancing –
and of life – is to enjoy every
moment and every step.

Wayne W. Dyer

Life is short. Kiss slowly,
laugh insanely, love truly
and forgive quickly.

Paulo Coelho

BIG DREAMS
OFTEN HAVE SMALL
BEGINNINGS.

CREATE A VISION BOARD
OF THE LIFE YOU WANT TO
LIVE AND KEEP IT IN VIEW
SO THAT IT INSPIRES
YOU EVERY DAY.

Laughter is the sun
that drives winter from
the human face.

Victor Hugo

IN DIFFICULT TIMES,
COME HOME TO
YOURSELF.

If you have good thoughts
they will shine out of your face
like sunbeams and you will
always look lovely.

Roald Dahl

Try to be like the turtle –
at ease in your own shell.

Bill Copeland

YOUR HEART KNOWS.
LISTEN TO YOUR HEART.

Give out what you most want to come back.

Robin Sharma

Whatever is going to
happen will happen,
whether we worry or not.

Ana Monnar

GIVE UP STRIVING
FOR PERFECTION.
OUR IMPERFECTIONS ARE
WHAT MAKE US UNIQUE
AND SPECIAL.

YOU CAN'T HAVE A
RAINBOW WITHOUT
A LITTLE RAIN.

Be happy with what you
have and are, be generous
with both, and you won't have
to hunt for happiness.

William E. Gladstone

If opportunity doesn't knock, build a door.

Milton Berle

Laughter is a sunbeam
of the soul.

Thomas Mann

SAY 'YES' TO
OPPORTUNITIES.

Laughing makes everything easier.

Carmen Electra

If you love life,
life will love you back.

Arthur Rubinstein

MOST OF THE THINGS
YOU WORRY ABOUT
NEVER HAPPEN!

Do what you can, with what
you have, where you are.

Theodore Roosevelt

SAVOUR THE LITTLE THINGS – STROKING A CAT, FEEDING THE BIRDS, GAZING AT THE STARS...

Release your struggle,
let go of your mind,
throw away your concerns,
and relax into the world.

Dan Millman

Laughter is magic
that dispenses clouds and
creates sunshine in the soul.

Richelle E. Goodrich

BREATHE DEEP
AND LET GO.

When you come to a
roadblock, take a detour.

Mary Kay Ash

Your attitude is like a box of
crayons that colour your world.

Allen Klein

SPRING-CLEAN YOUR BELIEF SYSTEM. WHAT YOU BELIEVE IS WHAT YOU BECOME.

The purpose of life
is to be happy.

Dalai Lama

Don't get your knickers in
a knot. Nothing is solved and it
just makes you walk funny.

Kathryn Carpenter

GIGGLING IS GOOD
FOR THE SOUL.

Most folks are about as happy as they make up their minds to be.

Abraham Lincoln

There are always flowers for those who want to see them.

Henri Matisse

DANCE YOURSELF HAPPY.
SALSA, FLAMENCO AND TANGO
ARE ALL FUN, SOCIABLE WAYS
TO LIFT YOUR SPIRITS.

Once you replace negative thoughts with positive ones, you'll start having positive results.

Willie Nelson

Real difficulties can be overcome; it is only the imaginary ones that are unconquerable.

Theodore Newton Vail

FOCUS ON WHAT
MATTERS MOST.

REVISIT YOUR CHILDHOOD DREAMS – TRAVEL, ACTING, WRITING A BOOK – AND MAKE ONE COME TRUE.

Laughter can bring
a new perspective.

Christopher Durang

If love is the treasure,
laughter is the key.

Yakov Smirnoff

NEVER
GROW UP.

The future belongs to
those who believe in the
beauty of their dreams.

Eleanor Roosevelt

FILL YOUR DAYS WITH PEOPLE
AND EXPERIENCES THAT MAKE
YOUR HEART SING.

BELIEVE
IN MAGIC.

Find ecstasy in life;
the mere sense of living
is joy enough.

Emily Dickinson

Aim for the moon;
even if you miss, you'll
land among the stars.

W. Clement Stone

LOVE PEOPLE,
NOT THINGS.

SPEND AS MUCH OF
YOUR TIME AS POSSIBLE WITH
PEOPLE WHO ENCOURAGE
AND SUPPORT YOU.

He who knows that
enough is enough will
always have enough.

Lao Tzu

The power of finding beauty
in the humblest things makes
home happy and life lovely.

Louisa May Alcott

MAKE HAPPINESS
A HABIT.

Your imagination is your preview
of life's coming attractions.

Albert Einstein

Happiness is when what you think, what you say, and what you do are in harmony.

Mahatma Gandhi

SING AS IF NO ONE
IS LISTENING!

Surround yourself with
only people who are going
to lift you higher.

Oprah Winfrey

The most important thing is to enjoy your life – to be happy – it's all that matters.

Audrey Hepburn

HAVE LESS.
DO MORE.

DON'T TAKE YOURSELF
TOO SERIOUSLY. READ A FUNNY
BOOK, WATCH A FUNNY FILM
OR GO TO A COMEDY CLUB.

Let your joy be in your journey –
not in some distant goal.

Tim Cook

SPEND TIME OUTSIDE TODAY. SUNSHINE BOOSTS LEVELS OF SEROTONIN, THE BODY'S 'HAPPY' HORMONE.

Let us be grateful to the
people who make us happy;
they are the charming gardeners
who make our souls blossom.

Marcel Proust

Happiness depends upon ourselves.

Aristotle

WHY NOT LIVE
A BIG LIFE?

LEARN TO MEDITATE.
A CALM MIND IS
A HAPPY MIND.

There are two ways to get enough. One is to continue to accumulate more and more. The other is to desire less.

G. K. Chesterton

GRATITUDE IS THE BEST ATTITUDE. THERE IS ALWAYS SOMETHING TO BE THANKFUL FOR.

Children are happy
because they don't have a file in
their minds called 'All the Things
That Could Go Wrong'.

Marianne Williamson

Until you make peace with who you are, you'll never be content with what you have.

Doris Mortman

A smile is a curve that
sets everything straight.

Phyllis Diller

FLOWERS IMMEDIATELY
BRIGHTEN OUR MOOD. PLACE A
VASE OF YOUR FAVOURITE BLOOMS
SOMEWHERE PROMINENT TO LIFT
YOUR SPIRITS.

The present moment is filled
with joy and happiness. If you
are attentive, you will see it.

Thích Nhất Hạnh

Now and then it's good to
pause in our pursuit of happiness
and just be happy.

Guillaume Apollinaire

DO NOT WAIT FOR
THE IDEAL CONDITIONS.
IF YOU HAVE A DREAM,
START WHERE YOU ARE.

EVERYTHING
WILL BE OK.

If you've got nothing to dance
about, find a reason to sing.

Melody Carstairs

Live life as though nobody
is watching, and express yourself
as though everyone is listening.

Nelson Mandela

The summit of happiness
is reached when a person is
ready to be what he is.

Desiderius Erasmus

NEVER STOP BELIEVING IN YOURSELF!

The best way to cheer
yourself up is to try to
cheer somebody else up.

Mark Twain

CREATE A GRATITUDE
JOURNAL AND WRITE DOWN
THREE THINGS YOU'RE GRATEFUL
FOR BEFORE YOU GO TO
SLEEP EACH NIGHT.

When the mind is pure,
joy follows like a shadow
that never leaves.

Buddha

MISTAKES ARE JUST PROOF THAT YOU ARE TRYING.

Cheerfulness and contentment
are great beautifiers.

Jennifer E. Smith

Happiness is found in doing,
not merely possessing.

Napoleon Hill

EACH DAY IS A
NEW ADVENTURE.

PUT LOVE INTO
EVERYTHING YOU DO.

If more of us valued
food and cheer and song
above hoarded gold, it would
be a merrier world.

J. R. R. Tolkien

JOY IS AN
INSIDE JOB.

There is no such thing as
the pursuit of happiness, but
there is the discovery of joy.

Joyce Grenfell

The soul's joy
lies in doing.

Percy Bysshe Shelley

CREATE MORE JOY IN
YOUR LIFE – FOLLOW THE
PROMPTS OF YOUR HEART.

Smile, it's free therapy.

Douglas Horton

LIFE IS BETTER WHEN YOU'RE SMILING.

If you're interested in finding out more about our books,
find us on Facebook at **Summersdale Publishers** and
follow us on Twitter at **@Summersdale**.

www.summersdale.com